Thanks for
everything,
Mr. McGarvey!

sincerely,
Kelli Plasterer
2006

#301

For Paul, who started it all
—C.D.S.

For A. & E. & C. with love
—R.T.

Handprint Books wishes to thank Mary Anne Iodice, MA, MPH, CHES, for scientific consultation.

Published in the United States in 2003 by Handprint Books
413 Sixth Avenue
Brooklyn, New York 11215
www.handprintbooks.com

First Edition
Printed in China
ISBN: 1-59354-005-1
2 4 6 8 10 9 7 5 3 1

41 thirst-for-knowledge–quenching poems by
**CAROL DIGGORY SHIELDS**

illustrations by
**RICHARD THOMPSON**

**HANDPRINT BOOKS** ✋ **BROOKLYN, NEW YORK**

Dear Miss Fullerton,

Science was my favorite subject back at North Shore School, and it was all because of you. After all, how many kids would actually want to stay after school to observe the feeding habits of cross-eyed flatworms or to draw detailed pictures of bread mold in a petri dish? I did, because you made science so intriguing and full of surprises. (Although my mother could have done without the surprise of 400 escaped fruit flies in our house—remember that genetics experiment you assigned us for homework?)

For many years I wanted to be a scientist. I even made up a poem, trying to decide whether I should be a chemist or a physicist or a biologist—or a teacher like you.

Astronomers are starry-eyed,
Botanists bloom around plants,
Zoologists go ape over animals,
Entomologists? Buggy for ants.

Meteorologists have their heads in the clouds,
Physicists quest for quarks,
Geologists rock, seismologists roll,
Ornithologists sing about larks.

Paleontologists get down and dirty,
Chemists overreact,
Behind a flask or in front of a class,
Scientists rule—that's a fact.

Well, it may seem a long way from science, but I became a poet—a poet who loves science. So I decided to try to combine poetry and science, and I am sending you the result. I have put everything (and I do mean everything—I hope you agree) students need to know about science into 41 easy-to-remember poems (and a few helpful memory-boosters). No more 25-pound textbooks to lug to and from school! No more memorizing! No more charts and graphs!

Thank you for the inspiration. Like the cell and its mitochondria, I am still "mighty fond of ya!"

*Your former student,*
*Carol Diggory Shields*

Some say there was a big, big bang—
Dust and gases swirled.
Gravity drew matter in,
And formed a little world.
Inside there was a molten core,
To keep it nicely warmed,
A mantle and a wrinkled crust,
Where peaks and valleys formed.

The miracle of water
Made oceans deep and wide,
An atmosphere of gentle gases
Shielded all inside.
A planet formed by changes,
And changes still to come,
A world that's very, very old,
A world that's very young.

# EARTH AND SPACE SCIENCES

# One World

Once upon a time,
The world was truly one,
The continents were crammed together—
I think that sounds like fun!
You could walk across Pangaea,
From Tahiti to Tibet,
Although there were no countries,
So it wasn't Tibet.
Yet.

# Fossils

Fossils tell of long ago,

About a world we'll never know,

Of reptiles soaring through the skies,

Giant palms and dragonflies,

Dinosaurs with beaks and bills,

Crowns of horn and bony frills,

Spikes and plates and fins like sails,

Twisting necks and thrashing tails.

Trilobites and fernlike trees,

Mountains covered up by seas.

In limestone, sandstone, chalk, and shale,

Fossils hold the ancient tale.

# Rock Doc

Three little rocks went to the doc.
The first said, "Doctor, please!
On the ocean floor, washed down from the shore,
I was squished and squashed and squeezed."

"Hmmm . . ." said the doc. "That's not a great shock.
You were just becoming a sedimentary rock."

The second said, "Doc, I was boiling hot,
Deep down inside the planet,
But then I was pushed, cooled off, and smushed,
And now I feel like granite."

"Hmmm . . ." said the doc. "Don't be a worrywart,
You've turned into stone of the igneous sort."

The third said, "Doc, I started as a rock,
Just like these other two,
I was under great stress, I'm a flattened mess,
What I am now, I haven't a clue."

"Hmmm . . ." said the doc. "Your condition's well known.
It's obvious now you're a metamorphic stone."

"Thank you, Doc!" said each little rock,
Wearing a happy smile,
Then one by one,
     they rolled out in the sun
And sat there in a pile.

# Home

Mercury's a pockmarked rock,
Venus is way too warm,
Mars is dusty; Jupiter
Is one gigantic storm.
Saturn's rings are full of ice,
Uranus has poisonous air,
Neptune's made of methane gas,
Pluto's cold and bare.

We'd better take good care of Earth
And treat it tenderly,
It looks like it's the only one
Just right for you and me.

# The Itsy-Bitsy Spider and the Water Cycle

The itsy-bitsy spider
Crawled up the water-spout,
Along came the water cycle,
And washed that spider out.
Out came the sun,
Dried up all the rain,
Which drifted high as vapor,
Forming clouds again.

The itsy-bitsy spider
Crawled up the spout once more.
The vapor soon condensed,
And down the rain did pour.
Out came the spider,
Who said, "You are insane
If you think that I will ever
Crawl up that spout again!"

# Going Up

Elevator going up—please step to the rear.
We're stopping at each level of our atmosphere.
Level One—troposphere; lots of nice fresh air,
Rain, clouds, sunshine—weather everywhere!
Level Two—stratosphere; the air's cold and dry,

(Watch out for ozone and aircraft flying by).

Level Three—thermosphere; hotter than a fire.

Level Four—exosphere; we can go no higher.

Hop out and view the satellites, orbiting around.

Step in now—this elevator's on its way back down.

# Inside of Old Smokey

Inside of Old Smokey,
All covered with snow,
Lurk tons of hot magma,
Gettin' ready to blow,
From deep in a chamber,
Up a vent to the top,
Like one great big zit that
Is soon going to pop.

The pressure keeps building,
And one day—KA-BLOOEY!
Out will blast lots of lava,
Red-hot and quite gooey.
Plus steam and sharp cinders,
Dark ash falling down,
If I lived near Old Smokey,
I'd get out of town.

MT. ZITTSAPOPPIN
10 MILES
←

From simple amoebas
To black-and-white zebras,
From algae to artichokes,
Jellyfish to swift gray sharks,
Lichens to mighty oaks,
Threads of life connected,
Each one to the next,
A fragile, ever-changing web,
Tangled and complex.

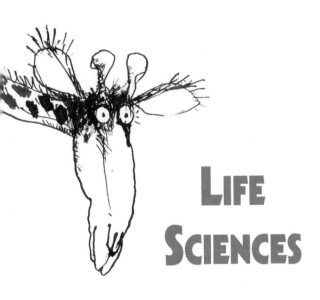

# LIFE
# SCIENCES

# Taxonomy

Let's hear it for taxonomy!
It tells us where we ought to be.

If you are a person, and not an azalea,
You belong in the kingdom "animalia."

Have a spinal cord? Your phylum's "chordata,"
A backbone too? Wow! You're a "vertebrata"!

Do you have teeth? Drink milk from a glass?
"Mammalia" is your appropriate class.

Have thumbs and ten fingers? Hey, pal, that's great!
Just like a monkey, your order's "primate."

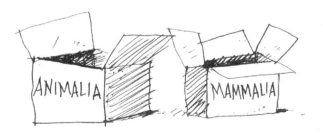

Do you walk on two legs? Step over here, kid,
Welcome to the family called "hominid."

What's your genus, my friend?
Well, "Homo" means man
(Including the good old Neanderthal clan).

The word "sapiens" means wise or smart,
And that is the reason that you are a part
(Along with your family and most of your friends)
Of the interesting species called "sapiens."

# Song of the Cell

Ladies and gents, I'm one of your cells,
I'd like you to meet my swell organelles!
Please meet cell membrane (kind of like skin),
She does a great job of holding stuff in.
Next up, cytoplasm, whose jelly-like juice
Keeps all my innards from sliding 'round loose.
And give it up now for my fine mitochondria,
Just gotta say, I'm so mighty fond of ya,
Always as busy as busy can be,
Turning plain food into pure energy.
My lovely round nucleus—so much to do!
If I had a brain, that brain would be you.
We're such a great team, and that's why we oughta
Go through mitosis, producing a daughter,
Who (thank you, dear chromosomes and DNA)
Will turn out like us, in every way.

# The Clone Zone

Are you feeling all alone?
Come on down to the new Clone Zone!
Bring along a cell or two,
And ABRACADABRA another you!
Someone who can do your chores,
Pick up the trash, and sweep the floors,
Take your place at work or school
While you relax beside the pool.
You and yourself, twice as much fun,
Today at the Clone Zone—
    it's two for one!

# Genes

Genes, genes, everyone's got 'em,

But not the kind you wear on your bottom.

These genes are the ones that made your nose

Look like the nose on Great-aunt Rose,

Or made your hair grow straight or curly

Or red like the hair of Cousin Shirley.

Some genes are shy, they're called recessive,

While dominant genes are more aggressive.

You got some from your mom and some from your pop

(You had no choice, no chance to shop).

Their genes mix and match, and when they do,

The outcome's a combo completely new.

So, unlike jeans on a clothing store shelf,

You're one of a kind—your own unique self!

# Directions

Bees tell other bees
Where nectar can be found
By flying to the hive
And dancing all around.

Each wiggle has a meaning
About where flowers grow.
I think that we should do this too,
When folks ask where to go.

"Turn right" is waggle, turn, and skip,
"Go back" is slide and hop,
"Go straight," three twirls; while cha-cha-cha
Means "Left next traffic stop."

# Fungus Among Us

There's a fungus among us,
It's everywhere!
In the house, on the ground,
In water and air.
You're sure to find fungi,
Sooner or later.
Just look inside
Your refrigerator.

# Ecosystem

Environment of creature:
Musty, dim, and dusty,
Draped with dirty laundry
That's getting rather crusty.
Peeling posters on the walls,
Loud music in the air,
Baseball mitts and soccer shoes
Decorate its lair.
Petrifying pizza crusts
Show its eating style,

Plus candy wrappers, apple cores,
And pop cans in a pile.
Judging from the evidence,
This could be no other
Than the ecosystem
Of my older brother.

# Evolution

With his "Theory of Evolution,"
Darwin started a revolution.
People were shocked! Disgusted! Appalled!
With the idea that we long ago crawled
Out of the ancient ooze and slime
To turn into humans, over time.
Then he claimed that monkeys were our kin,
Sending even more people into a spin.
Well, I think it's true, and I don't doubt it,
But I wonder how monkeys feel about it?

**Amphibian:**
"Eggs Taste Awful."
(Egg, Tadpole, Adult)

**Insect:**
"Eggs Leave Pupils Astonished."
(Egg, Larva, Pupa, Adult)

# Metamorphosis

A pollywog swam by a log in a bog,
On that log in the bog sat a great big frog.
The pollywog laughed, said, "Oh my, my—
You certainly are the ugliest guy!
With your bugged-out eyes and skin so green,
And the flappiest feet that I've ever seen."
The frog wasn't mad, he wasn't irate,
He slowly smiled and said, "Just you wait."

# The Platypus

Describe a platypus?
You're out of luck.
Fur like a dog,
Bill like a duck,
Claws like a lizard,
Venom like snakes,
Feet like a frog,
For swimming in lakes,
Tail like a beaver,
Eggs like a bird,
What is a platypus?
In one word—absurd.

**Photosynthesis:**
Chloroplasts take water and $CO_2$, turn them into glucose stew,
Through the phloem the glucose flows, out of the leaves pure oxygen goes.

# Meal Deal

When a plant is feeling hungry
And would like a little snack,
It doesn't have to buy a meal
Or bring lunch in a sack.
Doesn't call for pizza,
Or join the take-out line,
It just spreads out its leaves of green
Beneath the bright sunshine.
Takes a sip of water,
Breathes in some $CO_2$,
While chlorophyll gets busy,
Doing what it likes to do.
Cooking with the sunlight,
Fixing up a meal,
Delivered free throughout the plant—
Now that's a real meal deal!

I'm full.

# The Food Chain

The bug eats a leaf, the bug eats a leaf,
Heigh-ho, the food chain-oh, the bug eats a leaf.
A spider eats the bug, a spider eats the bug,
Heigh-ho, the food chain-oh, a spider eats the bug.
A duck eats the spider, a duck eats the spider,
Heigh-ho, the food chain-oh, a duck eats the spider.

The farmer eats the duck, the farmer eats the duck,
Heigh-ho, the food chain-oh, the farmer eats the duck.
The farmer stands alone, feeling pretty smug,
Thinks he's the top of the food-chain-oh—
Till he's bitten by a bug.

It started off as alchemy,
The search for what could never be,
Magical potions, riches unknown,
Gold from lead, the philosopher's stone.
But as they measured, mixed, invented,
Studied and experimented,
Something much better began to unfold—
They discovered true facts
Worth more than gold.

# CHEMISTRY

In 2002, an Illinois businessman built an actual
Periodic Table with different types of wood for each element.
It is used as a conference table at his company.

# The Periodic Table

The Periodic Table. Is anybody able
To make sense of those crazy little squares?

Numbers top and bottom, letters too, they've got them,
Not A-B-C, but scattered everywhere.

So iron's named "F-e," while silver's called "A-g"
And why the heck is "S-b" antimony?

Maybe I'm just dense; to me it makes no sense,
I say it's all "B-a" (stands for baloney).

It should be elemental, but my brain feels like a lentil,
And then they add in colors—it really isn't fair!

The Periodic Table. It's making me unstable.
Couldn't we just learn the Periodic Chair?

# What If?

Atoms are tiny, small as can be,
Far too small for us to see.
But scientists say that inside each one,
It looks like planets encircling a sun.
What if our sun and the planets that twirl,
Are only one atom in a much bigger world?

# Matter

Matter can be solid
Or a liquid or a gas.
Matter acts a lot
Like a bunch of kids in class.

In a solid, all the molecules
Are lined up nice and neat,
Sitting close together,
Each one in his seat.
(Just like in your class, of course,
Where not one kid is wiggling,
Passing notes or whispering,
Chewing gum or giggling.)

SOLID

Then it's time for recess,
And like solids melting down,
They tumble out the doorway
And down to the playground.
Both molecules and kids,
In clusters and in pairs,
Twirling, jumping, bumping—
Flowing here and there.

LIQUID

At 3 p.m., when school lets out, whoopee!
The kids just scatter,
Like molecules evaporating
Into gaseous matter.

But then on Monday morning,
They'll gather back at school,
Sitting in their classrooms,
Obeying every rule.

GAS

# Factoid

Carbon dioxide and iodine
Are weird because they both "sublime."
Without turning to liquid, each can pass,
From a solid solid to POOF! A gas!

# ANOTHER FACTOID

The molecules in soap hate water,
They hide out in the dirt,
This makes the dirt just float away—
And that's how soap cleans your shirt.

# YET ANOTHER FACTOID

Gas needs more room than liquid,
That's what makes popcorn pop.
When water inside it turns to steam,
The kernel blows its top!

**Signs of a chemical reaction:**
**1) Bubbles are produced. 2) Color changes. 3) Temperature changes.**
**4) Light is produced. 5) Water or other condensation forms.**

# Chemical Reaction

He was acid, she was alkaline.

He wasn't her type, but she thought he looked fine.

"You're opposites," warned her best friend,

"This will come to no good end!"

But they got together, mixed and mingled,

They bubbled and popped, frothed and tingled.

And when it was over, they both were gone,

Leaving water, salt, and this little song.

# The Solution Problem

My solution had a problem:
It was weak and too dilute,
I had poured in too much solvent,
And not enough solute.

So I added lots more solute
And stirred with concentration
Until, at last, it reached
The point of saturation.

But, oops, I overdid it,
No more solute would dissolve.
These solutions are a mystery
I fear I'll never solve.

"Heat it up," my teacher said,
So I did and—jubilation!
My solution's resolution,
Was supersaturation.

Lifting, shifting, slipping, sliding,
Pushing, pulling, rolling, gliding,
Energy, mass, and gravity,
Balance and velocity,
Forces moving things through space,
Forces holding things in place.
From galaxies to molecules,
Physics tells us all the rules.

# PHYSICS

# Tools

As animals, humans are rather wimpy,
Not fierce or fast, and kind of shrimpy.
We don't have claws, big teeth, or scales,
Tusks or wings or helpful tails.
So we invented gears and levers,
Wheels and pulleys, springs and cleavers.
Human beings are no fools,
We're not strong, but we have tools.

# Boyle's Law

Mr. Boyle, a very smart dude,
A law of physics he construed,

Under pressure, a gas
Will escape with a blast

(And sometimes with noises quite rude).

# Shocking

Walk on the carpet in woolly stockings,
You'll soon discover something shocking.
Especially when, quite innocently,
You reach for the door and touch the key.

ZAP!

Why does electricity (the kind that is static)
Have to be so darn dramatic?

The loudness of sounds is measured in decibels:
Whispering, 15 decibels; toilet flushing, 67 decibels; lawn mower, 90 decibels;
rock concert, 120 decibels; space shuttle liftoff, 200 decibels.

# Do You Hear?

Do you hear what I hear?

What you hear is air, my dear.

Air in waves, both high and low,

Spreading out like ripples flow,

Until they meet with your eardrum,

And then those silent waves become

Sounds of song, a trumpet's blare—

Music, truly, is in the air.

# Job Wanted

Hydrogen atom, fresh out of school,
Seeks work as part of a molecule.
Good team player, has one electron,
Would like to react and form a bond.
Whatever the compound, will get the job done.
Call: Atomic Element Number 1.

A compass does not point to the North Pole because Santa lives there.
It points north because the Earth is a huge magnet,
with a magnetic field that reaches out 37,300 miles into space.

# What Are We?

You can find us in your house.
We've got two poles, both north and south.
North to north we will not stick,
But south to north will do the trick.
We don't like plastic, wood, or glass,
But metal makes us hold on fast.
We keep track of your lists and chores,
And liven up those dull fridge doors.

hmmm.

# Gravity—It's the Law

Gravity's the law,
And you may not adore it,
But I can tell you, buddy—
You'd better not ignore it.
Without our good friend gravity,
We'd be in big trouble,
Your bed, your house,
Your dog, your cat
Would float around like bubbles.

Oh, it might seem like fun at first,
When nothing stayed in place,
But soon our very atmosphere
Would drift off into space.
You might not like it when you fall,
But listen to me, kid—
Obey the law of gravity,
And you'll be glad you did.

# Inertia

When you can't get out of bed,
'Cause your body feels like lead,
You're not a lazyhead—
That's inertia!

When you are skating home,
And your front wheels hit a stone,
You go flying on alone—
That's inertia!

On the land or in the ocean,
Isaac Newton's novel notion,
Applies to locomotion—
That's inertia!

# Roy G. Biv

Roy G. Biv,
Where do you live?
"Well, I'm a lucky fellow.
My home is full of colors,
Red and orange and yellow.
Streaks of green and shades of blue,
Indigo and violet, too.
When sunshine makes the dark clouds glow,
You'll see my home, it's a . . .
Rainbow."

# Science Project

Got batteries, screws, metal strips,
Connectors, alligator clips,
Switches, fuses, bulbs, and toggles,
Sockets, wires, pliers, goggles,
Colored wires by the dozen,
Which will get this buzzer buzzin',
Bells to ring and lights to light—
If I ever get this connected right.

# Title Index by Section

## Earth and Space Sciences

## Life Sciences

## Chemistry